THE GAME SAVIOR

Alisa McGrew Ross

The Game Savior

Copyright © 2023 Alisa McGrew Ross

All rights reserved. No part of this publication may be reproduced, distributed, or transmitted in any form or by any means, including photocopying, recording, or other electronic or mechanical methods, without prior written permission of the publisher, except in the case of brief quotations embodied in critical reviews and certain other noncommercial uses permitted by copyright law.

For permission requests, write to the publisher, addressed "Attention: Permissions Coordinator," at the email address below.

Email requests to alisa.ross.05@gmail.com

Ordering Information:
Quantity sales. Special discounts are available on quantity purchases by corporations, associations, and others. For details, contact the publisher at the email address above.

Published by Alisa McGrew Ross

Printed in the USA

First Printed, 2023

ISBN: 9798876839282
Independently Published

Dedication

This book is dedicated to my mother, Melissa M. McGrew-Ross.

TABLE OF CONTENTS

INTRODUCTION 7
UNFAMILIAR TERRITORY 15
LACK OF CONTROL 28
BURDENED 44
LOST AND FOUND 55
BITTER 65
SWEET 77
THERE IS MOM IN EVERY MOMENT 89
ABOUT THE AUTHOR 100

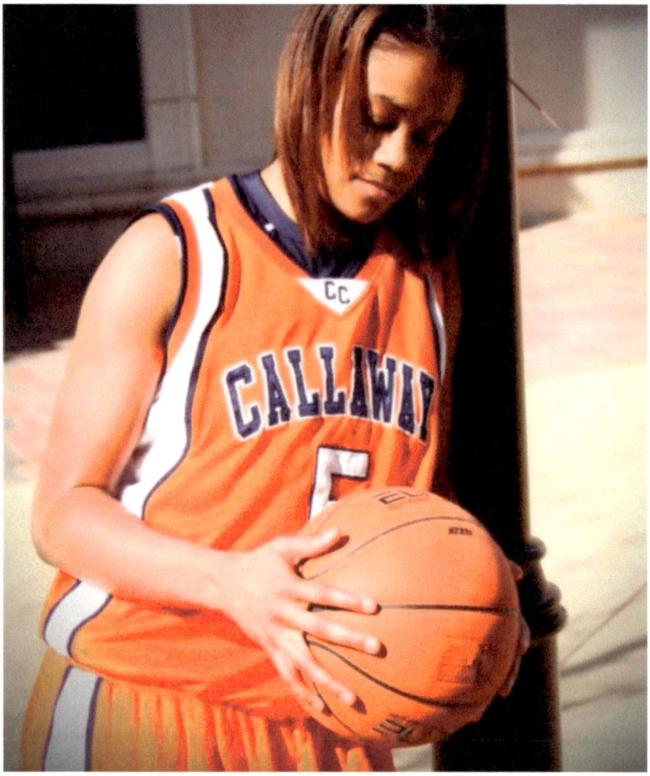
CC
CALLAWAY

INTRODUCTION

Tickets are being purchased and fans are entering the gymnasium for the biggest rival games of the season. As my team prepared for the competition in the locker room, I could smell the buttered popcorn and hear the chatter from fans amongst the electrifying music playing in the arena. With twenty minutes remaining prior to game time, I sat in my locker attentively, listening to my coach give her pregame speech. Shortly after, my team huddled to pray before exiting the locker room. My hands began to sweat, my heart began to race, and mentally the game had started. While standing in line awaiting the team's introduction, I began to pray for a successful performance and outcome.

"Dear God, thank you for waking me up this morning and covering me with your love thus far. Thank you for your many blessings today, one being the opportunity to compete in a game I love. Please cover me throughout this competition with great health and no injuries. Please allow me the needed capabilities to lead my team to victory. I pray that this game brings me great joy. I know I can do all things through Christ Jesus, which strengthens me. Amen!"

The team took to the court as the fans stood and welcomed us with great cheer. With twelve minutes remaining until game time, we completed our warm-up routine. During this time, I skimmed the arena for my mom and dad. My dad was present and on time, sitting courtside and engaging in conversation, but there was no sign of my mom.

The liveliness in the gymnasium had my adrenaline at an all-time high, and I was ready to execute. With no time remaining, it was time for tip-off. Both teams huddled at their bench and prepared for the starters to be announced. The commentator announced the opposing team's starters first and soon proceeded with my team. Eager and ready to dominate, I waited for the announcer to call my number. I was the last starter to be announced.

As I ran out to the center of the court, I heard the ringing voice of my biggest fan say,

"Alright, 5, let's go." I smiled, looking over my shoulder, knowing my mom had entered the building. She was fashionably on time in her number five apparel as she sat behind the bench, ready to cheer me on.

The scorer's table was set, and the referees were ready to officiate the four quarters of play. The whistle blew, and the ball was tossed up from the center of the court to start the basketball game. The intense play from both teams overwhelmed the court, which kept the game close in score. Several timeouts were taken by each coach throughout the game. With two minutes to play in the fourth quarter, fatigue began to take control. Both teams were exhausted from countless hustle plays, executed offense, and hard nose-in-your-face defense for the last thirty-eight minutes. I knew the only way to successfully overcome the game's last two minutes was to play with heart and discipline.

With the score being tied, both teams valued each possession. As the game continued, my team and I were down by two points with ten seconds to play in regulation. My coach used her last timeout to draw up the game's final play.

I sat on the bench during the timeout, drenched in sweat and hydrating, anxiously knowing the ball was coming to me. The fate of this game lied in my hands, and the last shot was being drawn up for me. Embracing the pressure of the moment, I looked behind the bench at my mom for reassurance, she looked at me and mouthed, "you got this". Walking confidently back onto the floor, I was prepared to carry my team to victory. The ball was taken out at half-court by one of my teammates and thrown to me. With nine seconds remaining on the scoreboard, a double screen at the top of the three-point line was set. I used the screen and shot a three-pointer, releasing the ball with three seconds left on the clock. After shooting, I looked back into the crowd for my mom, and her chair was empty. From there, everything went dark.

I woke up cold and sweaty from my dream, reliving one of the biggest games I had played. As I lay there in bed, my thoughts of how today would go overwhelmed me. I then remembered my aunt telling me to simply embrace the details of what today brings. I dreaded getting out of bed, knowing the time was near to say goodbye. I soon got up, gathered my things, and headed to my mom's house.

***

Every basketball game ends with a winner and a loser after four quarters of play, unless there is overtime because of a tie in score. Throughout my basketball career I learned many lessons that carry me through life but the one that helps me fight daily was given to me by my dad. Whether he was coaching or spectating from the sideline, before my games my dad would remind me to have fun, play hard every possession, keep the game close in score, and most importantly do not lose the fourth quarter.

1ST QUARTER
SHOW UP TO COMPETE

"I play to win, whether during practice or a real game. And I will not let anything get in my way and my competitive enthusiasm to win."
~Michael Jordan

Unfamiliar Territory

It was a sunny and warm Saturday morning. I stopped for breakfast on my way to the house. I knew my mom would not be standing over the stove cooking, waiting for me to arrive. As I pulled up to the house, I could see the kitchen window was empty of her presence, and it brought tears to my eyes. I wiped my face and pulled myself together before walking into the house where my brother and a few family members were gathered. I spoke to everyone and walked back to my childhood bedroom to get dressed. As the hour grew closer, I walked towards the front of the house to make sure everyone had arrived, and everything was still as scheduled. I received a phone call from my dad asking if he could change plans and meet me at the church instead because of rising family tension. I responded, telling him, "No! My brother and I need you here."

Everyone gathered outside, and we prepared to leave the house. We prayed and assembled for the last ride. My mom and I joked around on several occasions about making sure she arrived late to her own funeral. A joke then, but in reality now, she gave me a list of places she wanted to ride past for the last time. I kept my promise to her and created a route through the city of Jackson, passing by some of our favorite places where we spent most of the time. I remember sharing stories with my dad, brother, and nephew as we traveled through town with her body in front of us for its final ride. This moment brought tears to my eyes but joy to my heart.

We arrived at the church, where everyone was waiting. We unloaded the car, entered the church, and began services. At twenty-eight years old, with my nephew in my lap and my brother to my left, I sat in the reality of my worst nightmare, my mom lay in front of me in her casket. This was a hard and unexpected loss for my family. The celebration of her life continued as many people spoke of her great character, welcoming spirit, and loving heart. My nephew delivered one of my favorite words of expression as he stood saying, "I love you, Grammy. I miss you, Grammy. Grammy was a great helper. Grammy was a great prayer. Grammy was a great Jesus person. Now Grammy is baking for Jesus. Love Grammy Baby." He had written and practiced this speech all week so he could make his Grammy proud. I knew I had to speak the final words to give me peace of mind. Shortly after he finished, I approached the podium. I looked into the crowd and began to speak. I thanked my mom for being my example of true faithfulness to God, her unconditional love, and the many sacrifices she made for her family. The experience to give and receive her unconditional love will always be the biggest blessing in my life. I went on to talk about the many lessons she taught me about God, and my voice began to crack. I paused, wanting to cry. I remember feeling like God had failed me. As I closed, I promised to carry out her legacy by always trusting God, serving others, and becoming the best version of myself. I stood over my mom's body, embracing her for the last time. As tears rolled down my face, I told her, "I got this." I kissed her forehead and said goodbye. As my mom was being lowered into her grave, I stood thinking that not only was I motherless, but I was also without a best friend. This had all become so unfamiliar.

I was raised in a traditional two-parent household. I am the oldest child of three and the only girl. My mom was an educator for many years before starting her business, where she provided fiduciary services to veterans. My dad owned a lawn service and a construction business while also coaching basketball for teams I participated in. I spent most of my childhood days on construction sites playing in sheetrock, cutting grass, and mastering the art of basketball because I was such a daddy's girl. We were inseparable, and the many lessons he taught me over time became my means of survival. I enjoyed the hard labor in Daddy's world over cooking in the kitchen with my mom. As I grew older and my mom and dad divorced, my relationship with my dad changed.

Being a woman, I empathize with my mom more throughout the process. My dad and I still had a good relationship, but my mom became my best friend. We would talk daily for hours about everything and sometimes about nothing at all.

After graduating from college, leaving home and moving to Texas was a tough decision. I knew I would not have my mom in arms reach. I was not confident I could survive hours away without her physical support. My mom also expressed her concerns and did everything she could to ensure a successful transition. She helped me move out of state into my first apartment, where we created many memories. She traveled to visit me many times throughout the year. Her visits were the best because she would do all the motherly things every child enjoys; cooking, washing clothes, buying groceries, and ensuring all my needs and wants were met. Because I did not spend much time in the kitchen with her throughout my childhood, I spent many hours on Facetime learning from her as an adult. She kept me grounded spiritually, challenged me mentally, influenced me to choose right over wrong, and encouraged me to bypass the mistakes she had made. The loss of my mom has taught me to embrace the remaining time I have with my dad. Sometimes it is difficult because the love is so different, and it seems to never be enough. I hope to not sound greedy, but there is no longer a balance in the love I receive. My mom was nurturing, bighearted, gentle, kind, loving, and devoted to her family. My dad shows these things in a completely different way. I have chosen to adapt and understand that no one can love you more than they are capable of, including my dad.

My mom enjoyed celebrating birthdays. She turned fifty years old three months before her passing. She and I had planned her fiftieth birthday party, but it was postponed due to the rising cases of covid. I was living in Dallas at this time. I did not come home because she constantly reminded me we would celebrate the following week. Our birthdays were ten days apart, and she had planned to travel to Dallas and stay with me for a few days. It never crossed my mind that this would be the last time we celebrated another year of life together.

  I was excited for her to arrive at my home in Dallas. I welcomed her with a birthday cake and many gifts that she deserved. Seeing her smile as I surprisingly gave her some of the things she wanted warmed my heart. We celebrated by doing many things that week. The day of my birthday, I woke up to a well-written letter from my mom. She expressed how much of a blessing I was to her and how much she loved me always and forever unconditionally. She also gifted me a bottle of perfume that I had seen in the mall the previous day. She always knew how to make the day special. She never told me Happy Birthday before 3:16 pm, which was the time I was born. We had dinner at one of my favorite restaurants, and I ended the night with my twenty-eight birthday cake and my last happy birthday song from my mom.

My twenty-ninth birthday was one of my hardest days without my mom. I did not know it was possible to feel so abandoned. The birthdays were never about the cake or the gifts but had everything to do with her celebrating what she had birthed into this world. The day was long and never-ending. I worked until noon before traveling to Washington, D.C., with my dad to visit family. In some way, I expected my dad to make this day better for me, but this was one of many ways he and my mom showed love differently. I had talked to him several times throughout the day, and he forgot it was my birthday. It hurt my feelings and magnified my grief, but this was his character. Birthdays were never a big deal for him. It was not until 10 pm, in the airport, that my dad wished me a happy birthday. At that moment, I understood the difference in displayed love from each parent.

This brings me back to my dream from the night before my mom's funeral. I am experiencing the reality of her seat being vacant and adapting to no one being able to replace her presence. Although she is not physically here with me anymore, the many lessons and encouraging words she taught me over the years reassure me during the pressured moments of life. Releasing the ball with three seconds left in the game, I carried my team to victory against our rival. We won the game! Losing my mom has thus far been the biggest rival I have faced in my life. I walk confidently through all the pressures life brings, knowing I will win in life too. I hear her daily saying, "Let's go five; you got this."

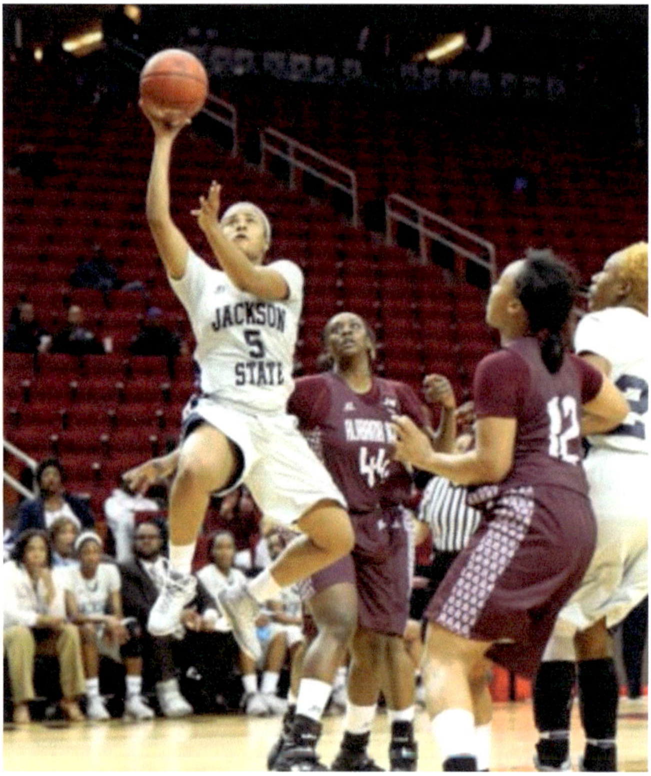
JACKSON
5
STATE
12
44

Lack of Control

I sat at work in my office on a Tuesday morning, frustrated with life. At the time, I was working in Dallas at a skilled nursing facility as the Director of Recreational Therapy. I was so irritated that I could not plan my workday. I needed to discuss how I felt with someone desperately. I called my mom, and she did not answer, so I sent her a text message venting about my issues. She said many things throughout the conversation that changed my perspective.

A message she sent that sticks with me read,

"You will allow the devil to set you up or trust God. If you do not want it to happen, do not speak about it. Only speak those things as if they were."

Immediately, I gained the mental strength to carry on throughout the day. I began to work, preparing materials for my sessions. Before leaving my office, I checked my phone. I received another message from my mom: "I have covid." I panicked, with overwhelming thoughts, responding "See, God got jokes. Do I need to come home?"

My mom having covid was disappointing to hear. She suffered from chronic Bronchitis, and I was unsure of the outcome because she had this underlying illness. After testing positive, she went home and quarantined. I began to worry and started making preparations to travel home. My mom was persistent about me staying in Dallas because I could not do much for her, and I did not need to get sick. My brother was staying with her and could take care of her needs. I called her by the hour to see how she was feeling and to make sure he was doing everything he could to make her comfortable. As the day continued, her symptoms got worse. It became harder for her to breathe, her body ached, and she had an uncontrollable cough. She survived the night but went to the hospital to seek treatment the next morning.

The hospital was over capacity and only had room for critical patients. All over the world, hospitals were in the middle of a crisis. The demand for nurses and direct care workers was at an all-time high. There were reports of some local hospitals treating patients in the parking garage, where they created additional space for care. I received a message from my mom describing the hospital's chaos and wait time. She mentioned that another patient had been waiting twelve hours and still had not been seen.

    I believe my mom's case of covid was critical, and she needed to be admitted. Still, she was treated with a Decadron shot and oxygen for relief before being discharged home. She qualified for an infusion because of her shallow breathing and chronic Bronchitis. Antibody infusion therapy works best if given a few days after a positive covid-19 test. The infusion can only be given without severe symptoms. Her infusion was scheduled two days after being discharged. She returned home and continued her quarantine, relieved of some discomfort. She was starting to feel better. I remember being on Facetime with her, joking and laughing about the scare of her having covid, thinking she had overcome the initial symptoms. By noon the next day, everything took a wrong turn.

The body aches, chills, and shortness of breath overwhelmed her. That night I did not sleep much. I stayed on the phone all night, in and out of sleep, monitoring her. My brother helped her in the tub, bathed, and put her in the bed, where she laid struggling to breathe. Her breathing had gotten so unbearable that she decided to walk outside to see if it would help open her lungs. My brother later found her in the kitchen, barely able to stand, he checked her oxygen, and it was severely low. He had contracted covid over time from caring for her, so he called my dad to take her to the hospital. This was early morning, the day of her scheduled infusion when she returned to the hospital. She was admitted with low oxygen levels and severe symptoms, disqualifying her from the infusion treatment she desperately needed.

My mom was admitted to the hospital on July 24, 2021, where she was treated for twenty-two days. The rules of the hospital were extremely strict during this time. Hospitals were not allowing covid patients' visitation until after ten days of quarantining, so she was alone. Because of the strict rules and overwhelmed staff, only one person could call and get updates. I was the designated person for all her medical needs. My mom was responsive enough to receive calls and texts for five days. We were constantly in contact with one another for about two days before her response became sporadic. I would Facetime her, with no exchange of words, and sit on the phone. Facetime was the only means of me being by her side. I made sure she did not need anything and received the best possible care from staff each shift. While we were on Facetime, I snapped pictures of us together because I knew my mom was fighting for her life, and these may have been some of our last pictures shared.

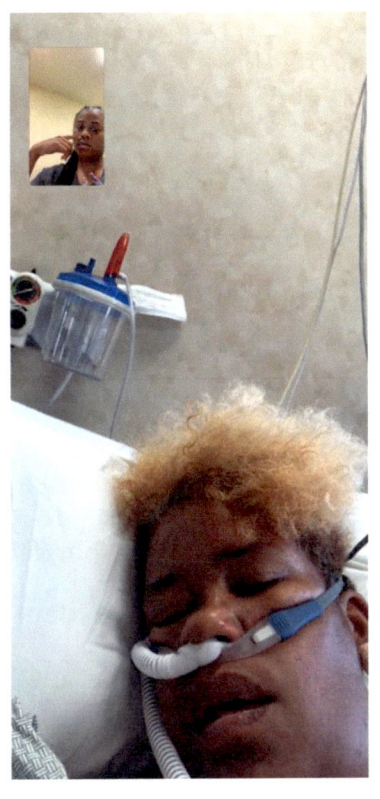

Days after she was admitted, her oxygen levels were still critical. She was treated with standard oxygen before needing high-flow oxygen than a CPAP machine, which was a non-invasive way of providing breathing support for her. The CPAP mask over her face made her feel so claustrophobic that she would not wear it for long. The mask caused her to become anxious, and she would pull it off her face. This highly disrupted her treatment, and she was not gaining enough oxygen. As time continued, she stopped answering my calls. She would instead send me text messages saying she loved me. The last message she sent was a single heart emoji.

    Early Sunday morning on August 1, I received a call from the nurse informing me that my mom would have to be intubated. She was not breathing well independently and was too anxious to wear the CPAP mask. A ventilator was needed for her survival. I jumped out of bed and began pacing the floor and crying, full of fear. The nurse gave me her personal cell phone number so I could Facetime my mom one last time before intubation. I called my aunt and brother on Facetime before merging my mom into the call. We had never in our lives seen my mom so scared. She cried fearfully while repeatedly telling us she was sorry and she loved us. With no words, my brother and I sat on the phone, crying. My aunt began to pray over her and for our family. My mom later became calm. She rested her head against her pillow and closed her eyes.

After my aunt finished praying, my brother and I said our last goodbye while she was responsive.

After that phone call, I sat in my apartment hysterical for days. The call repeatedly played over in my head. The fear on my mom's face and in her voice was unforgettable. These were the longest days of my life. I called the hospital for updates around the clock and kept a log of her reported vitals and medications during her stay. I obsessed over the reports, comparing them many times throughout the day. I needed hope, but there was none in the reports. My mom's health was not getting any better.

I read my Bible, prayed, and worshiped God constantly over the days. I journaled and wrote Bible scriptures on walls and mirrors throughout my apartment to keep me grounded in God's word. I found peace in doing these things. I refused to let my thoughts overtake me and decided to remain hopeful. Through this process, God revealed a hard reality to me: His Will must prevail.

I remember sitting outside my apartment enjoying the fresh air when one of my aunts called to check on me. She called often for updates on my mom and to see how I was doing mentally. During this call, I discussed the possible outcomes of my mom being critically ill. Not only did God reveal that His Will must be done, but He gave me a clear understanding that His Will could be my mom's restoration of health or death. I talked with my aunt about this, and she questioned my faith. She told me that I lacked faith in God's power to restore. This upset me! My mom's faith in God had carried me through many trials and tribulations. The one time she crucially needed me to stand firm with God, my faith was being questioned.

After sixteen days in the hospital, my mom's nurse called and told me she was allowed visitation. She had been moved to the critical care unit and was no longer contagious for covid. I had not talked to or seen her since we last Facetimed before she was placed on the ventilator. I was happy but scared to see her under these critical conditions. After receiving the news, I planned to leave Dallas and travel to Jackson the next morning. My mind wandered with thoughts about the severity of her health. The last thing I wanted to experience was someone calling and telling me my mom had died and I was six hours away. I became too anxious to wait until the morning. I packed my bags and traveled home late that night. The drive was long. I had many sleepless nights and was not well rested, but nothing was stopping me from getting home. I made it to my mom's house early the next morning, exhausted. I took a nap before heading to the hospital to visit with her.

    My initial visit to the hospital was scary. I was not sure what to expect. I had never seen anyone intubated or critically ill. I did not know how I would respond to seeing my mom alive but unresponsive. I became nervous as I entered the hospital and searched for her room. My heart raced, and I began to shed tears. I stopped at the front desk to check-in. While checking in, I introduced myself to the receptionist I talked to several times over the phone. She was always nice and outgoing. It was good to finally meet her in person. After we talked and I completed the necessary documents, she directed me to the back, where my mom was. Before walking into her room, I paused in fear. I soon gathered myself and entered.

    I finally stood alongside my mom's hospital bed. She lay there unresponsive, with her tongue partially out of her mouth and chapped lips. Her neck, hands, and feet were swollen tremendously from trapped fluid and lack of motion. She was covered with a hospital gown and had many IVs traveling through her veins. Several oxygen tanks sat near her bed. They were all connected to the tubes in her mouth, which stabilized her breathing. Many machines surround her, displaying the statical data of her health. There was medical equipment everywhere.

    Despite the disturbing visual of her discomfort, a sense of peace came over me. I was grateful for the opportunity to talk and love her. I could not stay the night at the hospital, but I was there until the end of the visitation period. I spent the next few days traveling to and from the hospital, embracing the last moments I had with her.

Days later, the doctor called my family to the hospital. He explained that my mom had set up pneumonia in both lungs, required one hundred percent breathing support from the ventilator, and her body was not able to sustain much longer. There was nothing else he could do. I could not believe what I was hearing. Making the decision between life and death was not for me to choose, so removing the ventilator was not an option. I refused to control the narrative and prayed to God that His Will be done. I informed family members of the updated report, and many came to visit her. I stayed at the hospital most of the day, except for going with my cousins to get food. We later returned that evening before the end of visitation. My mom was stable and had survived the day. My cousins and I stood around her, conversing about many memories we had experienced with her. While we were there, the nurse entered the room to give her medicine and rotate her stomach. We greased her bed sores she had begun to develop and cleaned her up before leaving for the night. I leaned over the bed and laid my head on her back as I left the room. I could hear the air from the ventilator being pushed into her lungs. I cried as I softly said, "I love you."

Around 5:00 am the next morning, my brother barged into my room, panicking. I woke up calmly, asking him what was happening. He explained that the hospital was trying to contact me. I had several miscalls from the hospital and my aunt. My mom had coded, and the nurse had started CPR. My cousin drove me to the hospital. En route, I received a call from the nurse. I hesitated to answer the call, knowing I was about to receive the worst news ever. Breathing with empathy in her voice, she stated, "Ms. Ross, we did all we could do. Your mom did not make it."

I got out of the car and sat on the curb, sick to my stomach. I cried as I told my cousin it was over. She had died! We walked into the hospital and sat in the waiting room with the rest of the family. We waited while the nurses removed the machines, IVs, tubing and cleaned her body. They later called us back to see her. I stood at the foot of her bed and mourned in disbelief.

The emotions in the room overwhelmed me. I walked outside to get some fresh air. While I sat there, I started calling others to inform them of her death. A couple of hours passed, and it was time to leave the hospital. Before leaving, I went back up to see my mom. I was back standing along her bedside one last time. I cried, standing there with a heart full of gratitude. I interpreted God's revealed truth correctly. I lacked control and placed my Faith in God's decision.

I prayed many days for the desires of my heart to be granted, which was restoration and great health for my mom, but this placed an expectation on God that He did not promise. I did not want to be let down by God because I expected Him to choose what I desired over what He saw fit. Once I received this revelation, I began to pray that God's Will be done.

My faith was not questioned. I knew the restoring Power of God. As I wiped the bloody residue from my mom's mouth, it was understood that God's Power would not be shown through the restoration of my mom's health but through overcoming of her death. Only being half the woman she was, many of her responsibilities became mine. A few days after her funeral, I sat on the bathroom counter in her room, contemplating life. I feared seeing everything she worked to build lost under my care. I sat there, knowing I had no time to grieve. Overcoming this season of life became my opponent. I had no strategy, lacked knowledge, and was broken but losing to life was not an option.

Burdened

While my mom was in the hospital, I was given a choice to resign or be terminated from my job in Dallas. I worked many days while my mom was ill because I became the primary source of income for both my household and hers. Once my mom had gotten severely sick, I could not balance my personal life and work. I scheduled a meeting with my administrator to discuss possible options for leave and job security. Unfortunately, the meeting did not go well. I had only worked eight months for the company and was not eligible for family medical leave. My administrator sat at her desk across from me, standing firm on policy. She was unwilling to work with me under these unpredictable circumstances.

Her response to the uncertain times we were living in brought rage over me. Before speaking, I sat quietly, looking at her, trying to find respectable words. I soon spoke, saying, "I only get one mom, and she needs me right now." I left the establishment with no thoughts of returning. It was not until my mom passed away that my administrator called and offered me my job back. With no source of income, I declined the offer. I could not move forward working for a company with low value and understanding for their employees.

I began searching for work in the Jackson area, applying for many jobs. I administrated my mom's estate and handled her personal and business affairs. I could not get many things done over the phone, so searching for work in Dallas made no sense. I soon accepted a job offer at a hospital in Flowood, Mississippi. I was grateful for work, but being back in Mississippi was unappealing. I was burdened with my mom's responsibilities and uprooted from the home I had created for myself in Dallas.

I was not mentally prepared for this new journey, but I felt like the survival of me and others depended on it. I worked long hours to sustain both households. I kept my apartment in Dallas, believing I could return to my regular scheduled life. My typical work day at the hospital ranged between twelve to sixteen hours. During those hours, I also found time to make important phone calls, schedule meetings, and help my aunt with my mom's business. My mom was a woman of great intelligence, intention, and preparation. She left me with everything I needed clearly explained and organized, but it was not all found in one place. It was up to me to locate and place the puzzle pieces together to close out her affairs. This allowed me to revisit our old conversations and think as she would. The process was stressful, but I gained much knowledge. I was reassured of how much she intentionally sacrificed for my brother and me daily.

My mom was very business-oriented, earning college degrees in business administration and accounting. Early in her career, she worked as an accountant for several companies. The hectic schedule and long hours required in the profession led her to a different career path. She became an educator, teaching high school and college students business courses. The change in profession allowed her more time with my brother and I. She was able to spend evenings, weekends, and holiday breaks caring for her family versus working. After teaching for a few years, she began exploring additional options to earn income and create employment opportunities. My grandmother often said, "Your money is in your hands." From this single statement, my mom and aunt created a business called HAANDS, which stands for helping and assisting needs daily somewhere. They used their knowledge, skills, and serving nature to support the needs of others. They offered a wide range of services such as; catering, transportation, respite care, homemaker, and fiduciary services, to name a few. Her business was successfully profitable and created many job opportunities as time progressed. I was familiar with my mom's business. I assisted her several times throughout her journey as an entrepreneur. Still, I never thought I would be responsible for the day-to-day operations so soon. I had so much to learn.

Not only did she create a business making a monetary gain by serving the needs of others, but often, she cared for people looking for nothing in return. She was selfless and sacrificial, carrying the load of others who surrounded her. I would always tell her, "Mom, you just let people use you." Usually, before I could finish the statement, she would rebuttal saying, "No one can use me. My blessings come from God, not from man. You never know what you are doing that keeps you blessed." Because of this, many people depended on her, including me. I had much of her character and many of her ways but not the same magnitude. How was I supposed to sustain this standard she set? I was lost in the shadow of someone who was everything to everybody. People no longer saw me for me.

My brother, Peanut, would jokingly call me "mom" from time to time. For a while, I could not find the humor in it from the perspective in which I stood. The dynamic of our relationship is great. We were raised to stick together and always have each other's back. There is not a large age gap between us, but the learning curve is massive. I had experienced a sense of independence before my mom died, but my brother had not. He was still Mama's baby. Because of this, I questioned if we could stand on our own as individuals after such a tragedy.

Sooner than later, life revealed the roles which we both played. Six months after my mom died, I was sitting at work talking with coworkers when I received a terrifying call. It was 1:30 in the morning when my brother called, saying, "The house is on fire; call 9-1-1." I panicked, rushing out of work in disbelief at what was happening. On my way to the house, I called my dad several times and could not get him. Of course, he was sleeping. Everyone was! I could not get anyone on the phone. I sent my aunt a 9-1-1 text, and she soon called and met me at the house. I began to cry, thinking the worst. I was unsure how bad the fire was and if my brother and nephew were alright.

I approached the house and jumped out of the car, asking for my brother's whereabouts. Fire trucks were parked outside, smoke was everywhere, and water hoses traveled throughout the house. There was no sign of my brother, so I ran into the house through the front door. I was stopped by an officer before entering. Before he could direct me, my brother yelled from across the street, saying, "Alisa, I'm right here."

I walked over to make sure they were alright. My brother stood there talking to our cousin, whom he had called over. My nephew sat in her car while we sorted through things. After everyone was safe and the fire was out, my brother began to report to the firefighter what had happened. He did not give many details. He reported that everyone in the house was sleeping before hearing the fire alarm. He found the trash can on fire in the laundry room and tried to put it out before exiting the house. Not much of this story convinced me, so I approached my cousin's truck and questioned my nephew. When I opened the door, he began to cry. I asked him what happened, and sure enough, he had set the house on fire. He lit matches, got scared, and threw them in the trash. I was at a loss for words. I returned to the house to complete the final walk-through with the officers. There was much damage, and the entire house was smutted with smoke. We were not able to stay there. I stood there distraught with a clear answer that we could not stand alone as individuals.

On every basketball team, a good leader is necessary for success. They lead by example by holding themselves accountable, lack selfishness putting the needs of others first, have strong self-worth and confidence in their abilities, and set high standards bringing out the best in everyone around them. My mom was our leader, and she was gone. In passing conversations, I would hear my brother tell others that I was just like her, strong and had everything together, but that was not my truth. I only allowed him to see this, being that leading under pressure was my nature. Unfortunately, I was chosen to lead in a game I never imagined playing. To finalize the report, my brother was asked, "Whose home is this?" Standing barefoot in his drawers, he pointed at me and said, "Hers." In those moments, I became burdened trying to balance being the cool older sister and a protective, nurturing mom.

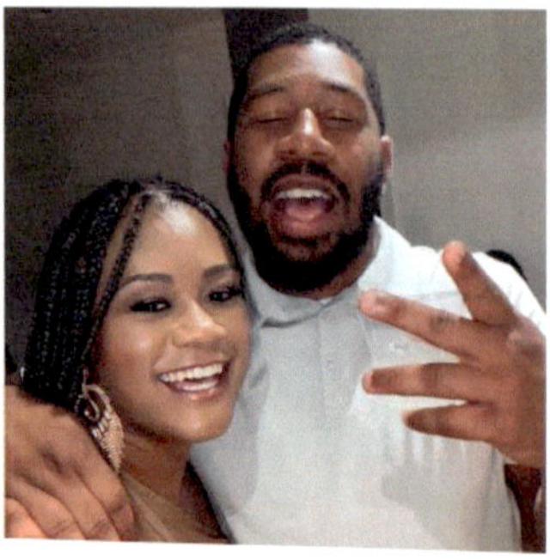
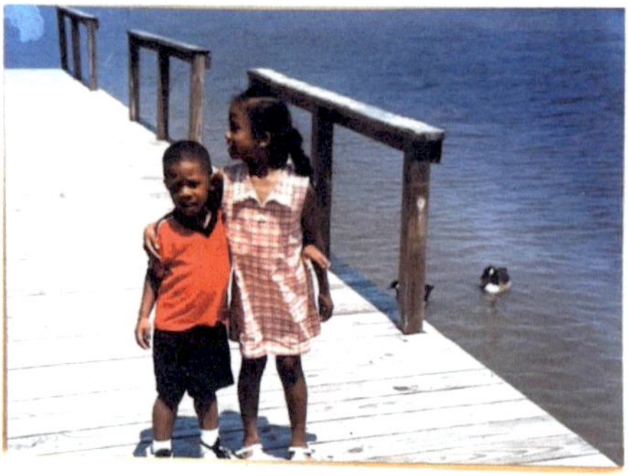
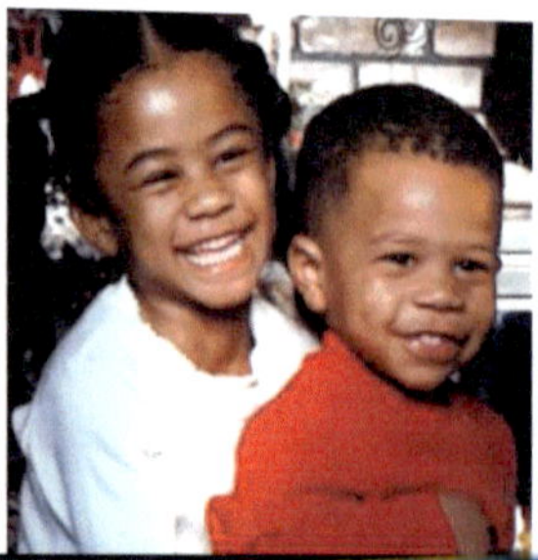
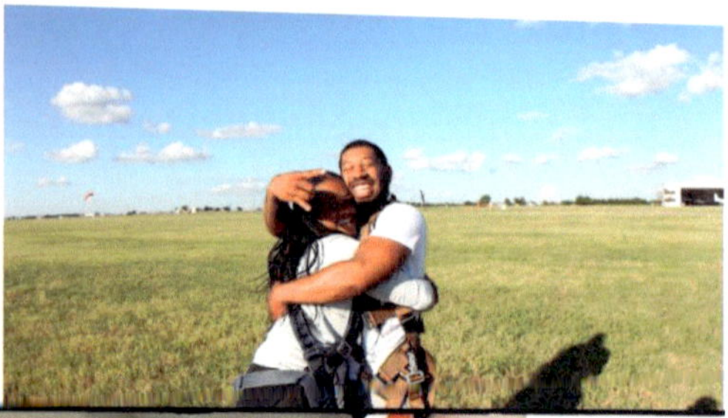
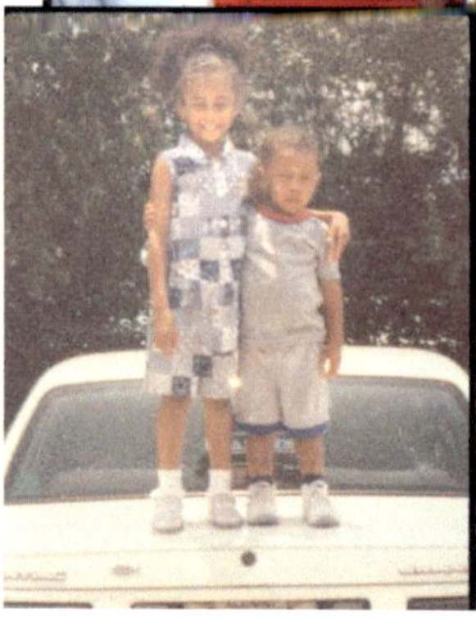
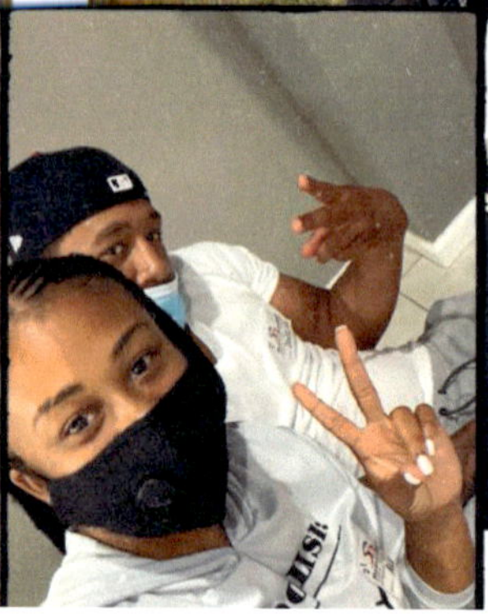
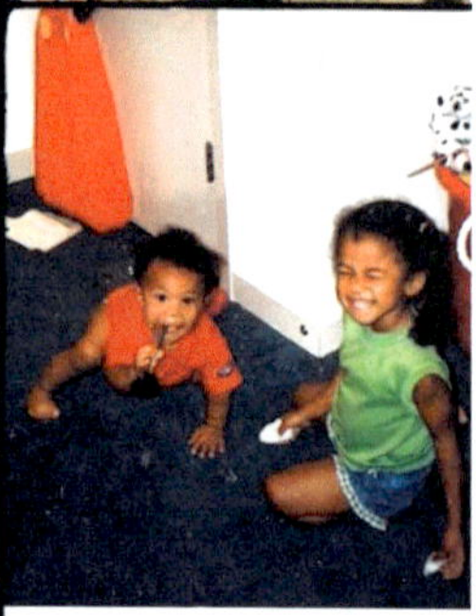

2ND QUARTER
KNOW WHO YOU ARE

"When you know both yourself as well as your competition, you are never in danger. To know yourself and not others, gives you half a chance of winning. Knowing neither yourself or your competition puts you in a position to lose."
~Sun Tzu

Lost and Found

I spent many weekends throughout the process of settling my mom's affairs, driving back and forth to Dallas. I lived there for three in a half years before my mom died, creating a home for myself. It was a sense of peace and a safe space to grow and establish my morals, values, and way of life. I spent a lot of time with myself over these years, which allowed me to get to know myself better without the standards of my parents choosing who I was. As a young child growing up, they laid the foundation for who I was supposed to be. Still, as I got older, I understood the decision of who I am is ultimately up to me.

My parents invested a lot of time and money and sacrificed much to ensure that I had everything needed for success. I spent much of my childhood in church, learning about God, being educated in the classroom, and becoming the best athlete on the basketball court that I could be. Choosing right over wrong in the eyesight of God was first. The church was a nonnegotiable in my household every Sunday morning and evening. I even spent Wednesday nights after school and basketball practice in Bible study, learning God's ways and principles.

Education was just as important to my parents. They spent countless dollars sending me to private schools during my early ages of development to ensure I received the best education possible before transitioning me into public school. I was an A and B student, bringing home more A's than B's. This was the expectation, and college after high school was not an option. They put a value on being career-driven and goal-oriented. They taught me to respect my elders, love and help others, work hard, and always be a leader, not a follower. Their standard is excellence in all that I do. The minimum has never been acceptable.

I believe I am becoming someone my parents would be proud of. I am not sure I could say this a few years ago, being that I was lost in the world, straying from the foundation they laid. I am my parents' first child, and living up to their expectations has always been important. All my life, I have attempted to honor them by living out their teachings, but at times I fell short of their standards. I was not a bad child that caused much trouble. I was respectful to my elders, kind-hearted and loving towards others, and worked hard to perfect everything I did. I exceeded the expectation of attending college by accepting a full athletic scholarship to a Division 1 University, where I completed my Master's degree while being a leader on the basketball court. I accomplished great things and led in many different roles that kept my parents proud. Still, there was one particular area of my life they did not approve of- my choice to live a homosexual lifestyle. I made this choice in high school, and without me having to have that conversation with them, they knew. This was a lifestyle choice for a decade. For that decade, I could feel the disappointment.

  Growing up, I was not the girliest of girls. Having tea parties, playing with Barbie dolls, and polishing my nails were never my choice of fun. Instead, I enjoyed my oversize gym shorts, sports bras with no shirt, and long adventures outdoors with my brother and boy cousins. I remember the joy of being at my aunt's house playing basketball in the street with the guys all day. On many occasions, I was the only girl amongst the pack of boys riding bikes, running football routes, turning flips on the trampoline, playing video games, and drinking water from the hole pipe once we had played enough. I was a different girl, a tomboy at heart. I loved myself and embraced my differences until, one day, I did not. I stopped appreciating the things that were different about me because they were the opposite of most girls. I experienced stereotypical questions from peers about my sexuality because I was a great athlete, and my image was that of a tomboy. I was never taught to fit in or follow others but feeling like I did not belong around the girliest of girls' made it convenient for me to choose a homosexual lifestyle.

During my freshman year in high school, other players on my basketball team introduced me to same-sex relationships. The emotional connection and physical experiences with a woman found me. Soon after, my interest in companionship with women began. I knew this lifestyle choice disappointed my parents, so I avoided conversations about it. I was going through what I like to consider an identity crisis.

For a while, I tried to cover up my interest in women by maintaining intimate relationships with both a boy and a girl. By my senior year, I chose to live in the truth. I left no room for stereotypical assumptions. At seventeen, I fell in love with a woman and openly made her my girlfriend for the next ten years of my life.

This lifestyle choice was devastating to my mom. It was something that she refused to accept, and it tainted our relationship. I can not speak from her perspective of raising a child that struggled with homosexuality, but my experience being a gay child was not great. I wholeheartedly knew that my mom loved me unconditionally, prioritized me in everything she chose, and wanted the best for me. However, most days, I felt like I was not enough and unaccepted because of my sexuality. I was forced to keep my relationship with my girlfriend in a box because it was so unwelcomed by my mom. She talked to me on many occasions about God's divine purpose for my life being the reason for her lack of support. She supported right in the eyesight of God no matter the situation. She often reminded me that God loves me, but He did not care for my lifestyle. She would always say, "No child of mine is gay." Was she right? Did I really know what I was, or did I allow the environment and the things happening around me to mold me into something I was not?

It was not until I moved to Dallas that I began to discover who I was. I lived there with my girlfriend, which allowed me to be more free in my sexuality without the opinions of others. I had no family in Dallas, so I was alone in my own space when I was not with her. I was able to process past traumas, unlearn generational behaviors, and decide who I was at my core. I had time to address my whole person without any influence. Soon after, I began to evolve. My heart began to grow more and more in agreement with God's law. I became torn between being right with God- striving towards His purpose for my life or staying committed to my fleshly desires. My relationship had its ups and downs, but I enjoyed it and never imagined my life any other way until I was spiritually convicted one day. This conviction was so powerful that it gave me the courage to walk away from the ten-year lifestyle.

I was never a fool to my mom just a growing child making mistakes. She was a proud parent to hear that I was ready to choose my faith in God over my fears and insecurities. In many ways, I am the same girl as my childhood. My hobbies and tomboyish nature remain, all while mastering my femininity. I have learned to embrace those things about me without any pressure of comparing myself to other women. My mom reminded me I would always win if I sustained my identity in God. After she passed, I found many of her written prayers asking God to give me strength and courage to stand up for what I know to be right and to release me from the sins of the world. She prayed for God to send me a Godly husband that loves me and many blessings over my children. One of the greatest things I gave her before she died was peace in becoming who she always knew I was by submitting to God's way despite my desires. Unfortunately, I became motherless before becoming a wife or a mom. I lost precious moments with her because I chose to live outside God's purpose and not know who I was. Moments that I will never get back.

Bitter

As a young child, I experienced the negative impact death could have on people. An impact that changed the dynamic of not only my extended family but my nuclear family as well. In February 2007, my dad unexpectedly lost his father to a massive heart attack. My Grandad's death and the mishandling of his estate caused division between my dad, his siblings, and my grandmother. A division so great that it has yet to be resolved years later. It was a hard loss for my family.

My dad did not cope well with his father's death and family chaos. He was hurt and began searching for fulfillment in all the wrong places. Sooner than later, his decisions began to affect his household. He and my mom started having marital issues, eventually affecting my brother and me. Things for us became uncommon. My parents began sleeping in separate rooms, my dad's presence at home began to lack, and my mom shed fewer smiles and more tears regularly. My parents tried to hide their issues from us as best they could, but unfortunately, after a while there was nowhere else left to hide.

February 13, 2009, my brother and I received the news we never expected. It was a Friday I will never forget. I had a basketball game at my high school that night. My mom and brother were in the stands, but my dad never showed up for the game. That was unlike him. Once the game was over, I received a message from my mom stating that she would be waiting in the car so we could leave. After reading her message, I wondered if something had happened. It was very rare that we did not stay and watch the boys' team play. I got dressed, grabbed my things, exited the locker room, and proceeded to the side door to leave the school. My mom parked in the street with her emergency flashers on, waiting for me. I walked down the sidewalk towards the car. My brother was sitting in the front seat, so I opened the back door and got in. I spoke once I entered the car, but immediately after, I asked about my dad's whereabouts and why he was not at my game.

With tears in her eyes, my mom replied, "he will meet us at home."

There was little conversation during the car ride as we traveled home. I sat in the back seat looking out the window, bothered by my mom's sadness. We soon arrived home. With so many unanswered questions, my brother and I entered the house and began settling in for the night. My dad had not yet made it home when we got there. I was relaxing across my brother's bed on the phone. He was playing his video game when we heard my dad's hard-bottom shoes clacking against the wood floor as he walked down the hallway to the back rooms. I raised from the bed and looked over my shoulder towards the door frame awaiting his presence. He stuck his head in my brother's room and greeted us before walking next door into his bedroom and shutting the door.

My brother and I continued on with what we were doing. Some time had passed before my dad came from his room and asked to speak with us. My brother paused his game, and I got off the phone immediately. We then followed my dad down the hallway to the living room. I was unsure what he wanted to discuss with us, but I knew it was not good when my mom walked in from the kitchen teary-eyed. We all sat down to talk. My parents sat in the end chairs across from each other, and my brother and I sat on the couch between them. My dad turned the television volume down and began to speak. Before he could get many words out, my brother and I began to empathize with my mom's devastation, unaware of what had happened. I watched the tears start coming down his face as I tried to gaze off and withhold mine.

As my dad continued to speak, he talked to us about the obvious martial issues he and my mom had been experiencing. He stated that he had done something wrong. He then began to tell us that he was involved in an affair and had created a life in the midst of it. I had a day-old baby brother named Ashton that my mom did not birth. Looking over at him, I could no longer withhold my tears. I could not process what I had been told. I believe I was as hurt as my mom after hearing this. Before ending the conversation, my dad reminded us that he was not God; he made a mistake and assured us that he and my mom would be working through things. Without many questions or much to say, I left the room, telling my dad I could never forgive him. For the remainder of the night, I lay in bed crying until I fell asleep.

My parents stayed married years after my dad's affair and love child. My mom welcomed Ashton into our family as if she had given birth to him. Whenever he was at our home, she nurtured him as if he were hers. So much so that he identified with her as a mom, just as my brother and I did. She always taught us to love and to treat him no differently than we did each other. This new dynamic in my family was hard to accept. Still, my mom was willing to work through things, so I supported her the best I could despite the feelings I experienced. As a family, we never discussed much else about what had happened. Still, daily, my brother and I experienced change within our home. It was an emotional rollercoaster in my household from this point, leading to my parents divorcing.

I was a sophomore in high school when I learned about my dad's affair and in my early 20s when my parents decided to divorce. I was young and unaware of how to respectfully address my emotions unapologetically. My dad would often tell my brother and me that his and my mom's relationship had nothing to do with us, so I never felt the need to express my frustrations, anger, and pain. Instead, I bottled it within and dealt with it as best I knew how. As I matured and began to better know myself, I understood the effect of all I had experienced. I started to open up and address my feelings with my mom; surprisingly, she welcomed them. I even had negative feelings towards her for some of her decisions. She never got defensive but instead gave me her reasoning for her actions and was okay with me disagreeing with her. The conversation was easy to address with her but not so easy with my dad. I was most afraid that he would feel attacked and try to justify himself while I needed him to simply listen. I continued to bear the burden of my feelings until, one day, I became desperate for healing.

Ironically, a year before my mom passed, I wrote a letter to my dad expressing my deepest pain, hoping it would release me from the emotional prison I was living in. I found freedom in the truth and gained my first step toward healing in writing to him. I explained my unconditional love and trust for him and never imagined that it could be broken. He was my first love as a little girl, but also my first heartbreak. A heartbreak that I would always be reminded of from the person I trusted more than anyone. I discussed feeling betrayed and the insecurities it welcomed. My dad could not have considered me in his choices, and the effect of this is the constant question of why I was not enough for him to choose differently. He often made statements regarding keeping me under him growing up to save me from the guys. Still, while protecting me from everyone else, he failed to protect me from himself. I did not appreciate my mom hurting, and everything I knew my family to be had been taken from me at once because my dad was hurt, and I decided it was all about him. While writing this letter to my dad, my heart opened and created room for forgiveness. So I did something I never said I would do; I forgave him. I learned that forgiving him was not all about him but was most beneficial for me to move on in life. I wrote to him expressing my acceptance of him being flawed, and through the deepest of pains, I will always love and look forward to caring for him in old age.

My hard truth is that I question why God chose to take my mom first over my dad. Many may agree that this is harsh thinking, but my freedom is in the truth. I fight with this thought often, not because I love him less but because I imagined a different ending to my mom's story. In many ways, her death questioned if I truly had forgiven my dad for his past wrongs. The real you comes out in painful moments. I have learned that God often allows pain so that you can see yourself and others. My heart was being revealed. The pain created a bitterness I never knew I could possess. One which my dad may have experienced when his father died. I can better understand his grief now that I am experiencing the death of a parent, but I will never validate how he chose to cope with his pain. In the letter that I wrote to my dad, I said, "You are a broken person, and you must deal with that part of you. Someday your pain will become the source of your strength." I find myself reading these words over and over to myself as I stand now in a season that was once his- choosing who I will be in the face of indescribable pain.

3ᴿᴰ QUARTER
MAKE THE NECESSARY ADJUSTMENTS

"The ability to adjust is the entire game."
~Unknown

SWEET

Momentum is a commonly used term in basketball. The idea is that two opposing teams work to capture the flow of the game. A team with great momentum is really on the move- meaning they are defending their opponent well, getting stops on defense, all while creating offense for themselves and making shots to control the game. A team with great momentum is hard to stop. The teams must know their identity through the many momentum shifts of the game and remain disciplined in that. Choosing to adapt to the opposing team's play, forgetting who you are, and failing to make the necessary adjustments often result in loss.

Showing up to compete or knowing who I was after the loss of my mom was not the hardest part of the game for me. My biggest struggle was making the necessary adjustments to keep the score close. It was painful to watch others navigate through her loss so easily as I simply existed in my grief and focused on making others around me comfortable. No, I did not expect life to stop, but everything was changing too swiftly for my liking. Everyone was choosing what was best for themselves, and I failed to do so.

On Thursday afternoon in mid-November, I received a call from my dad while working at my desk. After greeting me, he said he would like to ask my brother and me something important. He asked if we preferred to sit down and talk together or if the dynamic of us speaking mattered. Of course, I was eager to know what was going on right away, so I told him to consult with my brother later. Using the side door connected to my office, I walked outside. It was a cool and sunny day. I walked to the playground and sat on the swing in the open field while conversing with him. I found myself swinging and enjoying the breeze while I listened. He soon went into his reasoning for calling and later asked for my thoughts on him possibly getting remarried. Instantly, I dragged my feet in the dust to stop the swing. Before coming to a complete stop, I jumped from the swing and began to pace. I did not want to react with emotions, so I just held the phone without responding to gather my thoughts.

My dad asking my thoughts on him marrying another woman came at the worst time ever. My thoughts were not great. I had just buried my mom three months prior to this conversation, and personally, I was in a dark space. Life was not only getting the best of me, but I also was experiencing the first traditional holiday season without my mom. I enjoy watching love unfold, and marriage is a beautiful thing. Still, I selfishly said I alone need my dad in this particular season of life. A marital union is sacred. I was raised on God's teachings, so I understood that marriage creates a hierarchy. Once a man is married, his commitment to his wife is the first priority, and his commitment to his children follows.

I was not okay with this. Aside from my mom, I could not process another woman being placed before me in my dad's life. Their union was all I had ever known. My parents were high school sweethearts who dated each other for many years before getting married in December 1993. They had been married 24 years before divorcing. Afterward, they maintained a friendship that created room for family dinners, gatherings, and outings to remain as they were. The finalization of their divorce and the reality of their relationship left things unclear to me as a child. I never experienced seeing my mom with any other guys, and there were only two occasions I experienced seeing my dad with someone other than my mom. I was familiar with him dating someone but never to the extent of him possibly getting remarried. As dysfunctional as my family was, the reconciliation of my parents was always ideal for me. I never considered the question of remarrying someone new being asked by either of them, but there I stood.

After awkwardly holding the phone for some time, I began to speak. As badly as my heart wanted to speak from the griefful space I was in, I chose not to. Instead, I responded from a place of understanding, support, and gracefulness because I knew this was the person I wanted the pain of it all to mold me into. I began questioning him on whether he was wholeheartedly sure of remarrying someone else or if the circumstances of life were making this decision for him. He rebuttal saying, "I just want to get things right, and this is a second chance for me to do that." My heart ached, and the rage brought tears to my eyes while he spoke about this. All I could think about was the second chance to get it right my mom was not getting and the things she endured within their union. As I stood there listening to my dad speak, God reminded me of the second, third, and fourth chances he allows me daily. Because of this, a graceful spirit became my responder to him. I assured him that he was not the only person experiencing a second chance in life to be right; I was as well. As our conversation ended, I gave him my blessings on getting remarried and asked him to honor it by being his best self. Not just for his new wife but for me as well- by becoming the example of a man to a woman I know he can be.

My dad proposed on Christmas Day that same year. As expected, his fiancée said, "yes." Although I wished him many blessings in his new marriage, I knew deep down that my heart was not yet open to actually accepting this change. My dad's fiancé tried to bridge the gap of this new transition by asking me to be in the wedding but I could not. I had to decline. I was unsure how to support my dad's desires without feeling like I was betraying my mom and losing my family. I never imagined life being like this. I had no momentum in this game anymore, forcing me to reevaluate the changes I needed to make to overcome this defeat.

As surreal as life felt for me, it was not. Everything happening was real. The adjustment I needed to make in life had everything to do with radical acceptance, which is letting go of the need to control, judge, or wish things were any different than they were. I had to change my mind and stop living my life as if my mom was still alive to give hope to my purpose, goals, and desires. It was clear that life would not wait for me to be ok, so I had to intentionally incorporate practical tools to help me overcome. I began showing up for myself by doing the necessary work in Psychotherapy, creating boundaries, praying, fasting, and choosing my own happiness. Practicing these things became a huge playmaker for me. It created room for me to address the past yet embrace the present moments of life with joy and less guilt. As I sat in the front of the church on the day of the wedding, trying to hold onto what was, I knew it was time to let go.

This bittersweet moment of hearing my dad say I do is where I gained back control over my life; by accepting that reality is what it is, understanding that the situations in my life causing the pain have a cause, and knowing that life is still worth living through all that I endure.

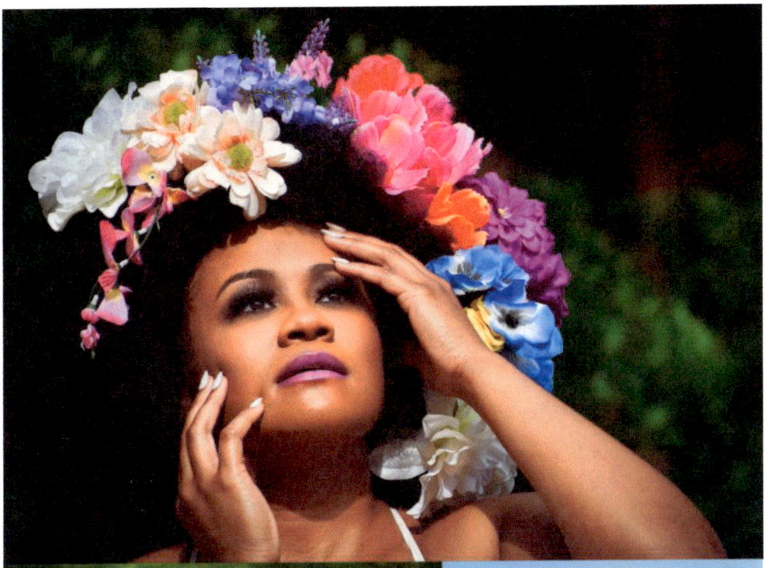

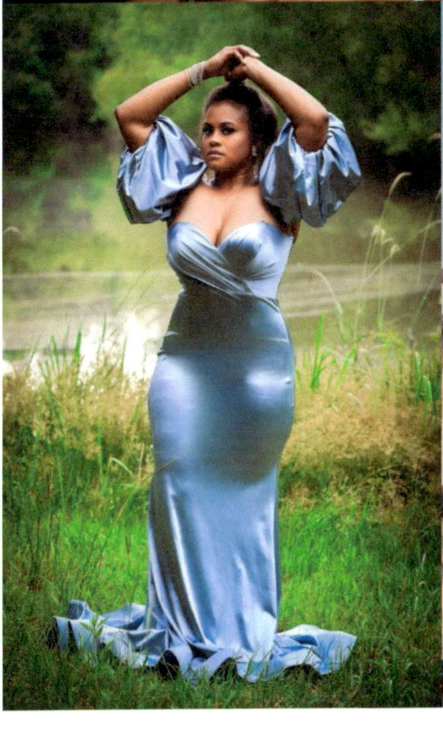

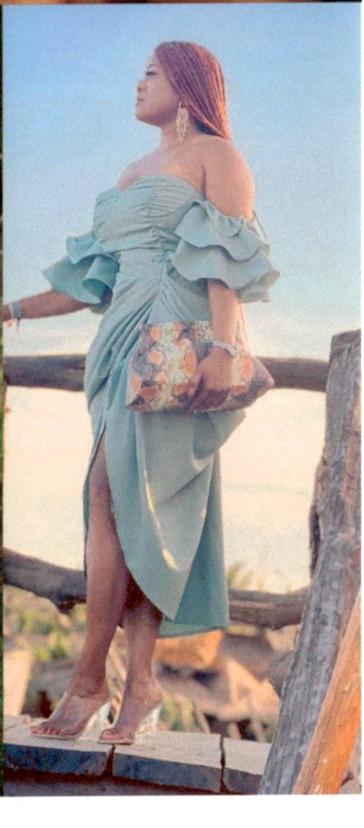

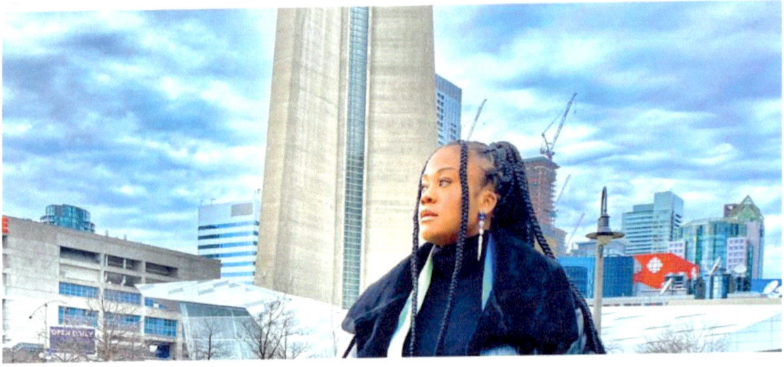
OPEN DAILY

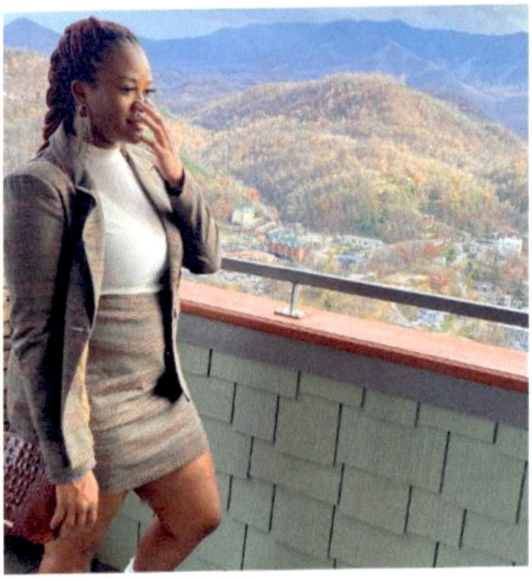

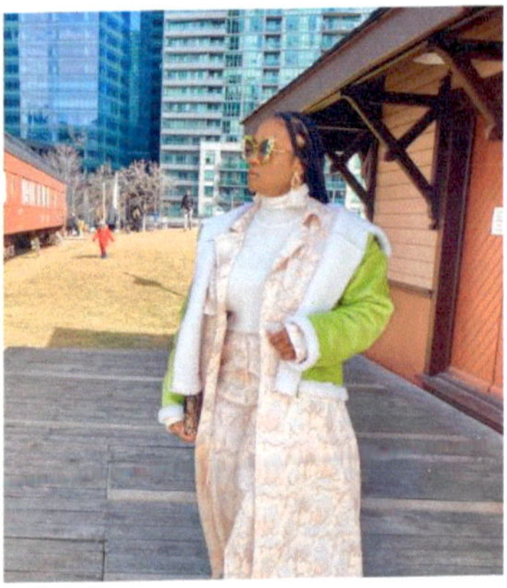

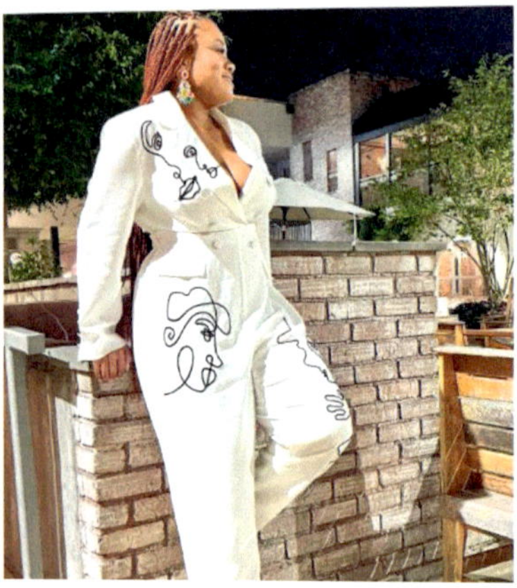

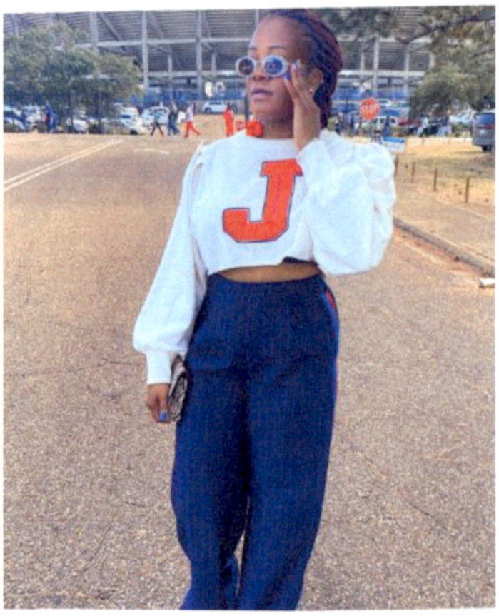
J

4TH QUARTER
DO NOT LOSE

"Winning and losing does not have any meaning, because some people win by losing and some lose by winning."
~Unknown

THERE IS MOM IN EVERY MOMENT

August 15, 2022, was my mom's one-year death anniversary. That day, I traveled midday to the cemetery to visit her grave. In a basketball game, timeouts are allowed. This is a period of time during a game in which the game is temporarily stopped, often to allow the teams to make adjustments or substitutions and for coaches to give instructions to their players. During this short timeout period, the players report to their assigned sideline, where they meet their coaches. In the midst of this game with life, my mom's gravesite is my sideline. I go there not only to find peace in my decision-making or talk through the adversity that life throws at me but to also celebrate the big plays I execute within this game. When I arrived, I got out of my car and began to walk up the hill to her grave. I remember feeling like I was ready to throw in the towel and quit as I looked back over my shoulder, outside of the cemetery, at my opponent- life. I had done all I knew to do thus far to sustain myself physically, mentally, and emotionally. Still, I found myself down in score because nothing filled the void in my soul from her absence.

My mom always challenged my perspective when things did not go as planned in my life. She would ask, "Is the glass half full, or is the glass half empty?" She intentionally found the blessing and praised God through the negative things she endured. Throughout her lifetime, what I processed as losses she embraced as God's Will for her journey, even when it was painful. I could not spiritually process how God was moving in my life, and this is where I was losing. As I sat at her headstone in the midst of life, "life-ing," I could only remember my mom and what I believed she would say to coach me through this journey and they are as written.

If it is not fatal, then it is not final. I know you never imagined losing me, and neither did I think I would be gone so soon, but it is okay. I understand that my death hurts deeply, but you must trust that God makes no mistakes. We made many plans for the future, but it is time you let go of those and simply embrace the memories we shared over the years. Being a mom was one of God's greater gifts to me. My firstborn, one of my three heartbeats, you must move on from here. Be sure to take your brother with you on this journey, and know that you guys choosing to live and not only exist is how my legacy continues.

Protect what I have built thus far and continue to build for future generations. Keep your heart open to forgiveness and always lead with love because God is love. Every day, choose grace and love towards your dad. Although things did not work out with us as you may have hoped, know that God has the power to heal that wound. Enjoy the remaining days because one day, God will take him physically from you as well. Allow yourself to be vulnerable to those things you are scared of, and when God blesses you, remain humble by always choosing to be a blessing to others. I hope joy, happiness, and unconditional love find you and that God blesses you beyond your dreams. Open your heart to God, and do not become angry with Him for what He has chosen for me.

I have sat in many arenas and watched you help win many games for your team, but you will never win against life in your own strength. Understanding that my death did not only happen to you, but most importantly, it happened for you is how you win this game with life. The pain in your grief allowed by God is the true beginning of you losing yourself and finding comfort in His plan.

The birth of your becoming will be the blessing that comes from what you have identified as the worst part of your life. I will watch over you every step of the way as you continue on. Take less time longing for me and live- that I may live on. Dry your eyes, hold your head up, and give life your best as if you are my child. Stay beautiful inside and out. I love you always.

God has an incredibly beautiful way of destroying the old without harming the new and even growing, strengthening, and establishing us in the process. The very thing that shattered my heart into pieces also happens to be the thing that saved my soul. After opening my heart and finding my mom's words, I understood that the dead no longer wanted me to live a dead life. There is Mom in every moment, which brings me great pain, but knowing God is bigger than the moment allows me to rejoice over the new He is building. At the end of every game, there is a winner and a loser. Whenever my mom looked up at the scoreboard in her game of life, she always knew she had won, even when physical circumstances showed she had lost. She knew she had a savior in God. I sleep peacefully at night, knowing that she won her game of life by being faithful to Him. Trusting God, His Will, and following His plan for my life is the play that saves the game and keeps me victorious.

To God be the Glory is how my mom's game ends, and mine continues.

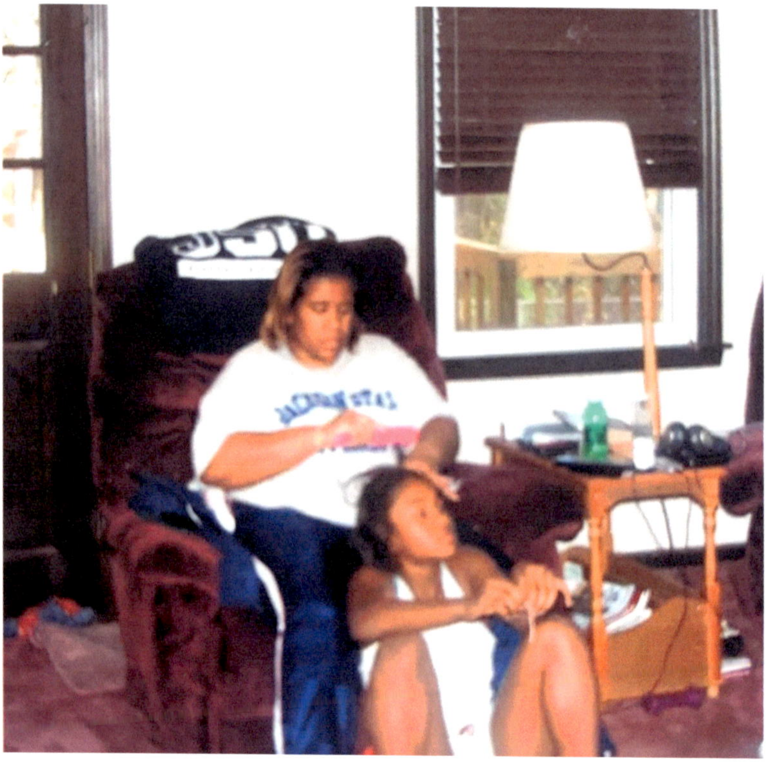

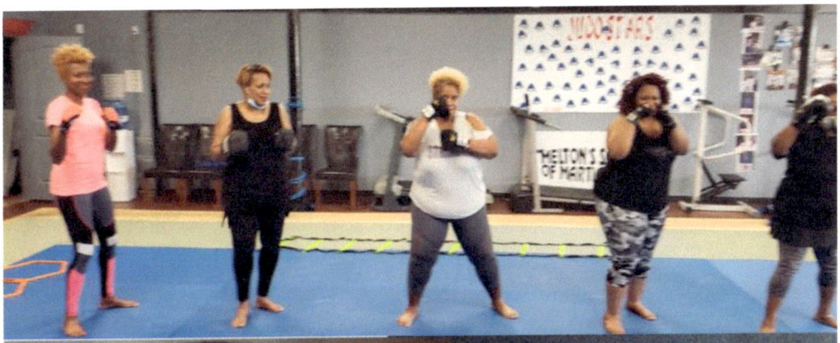

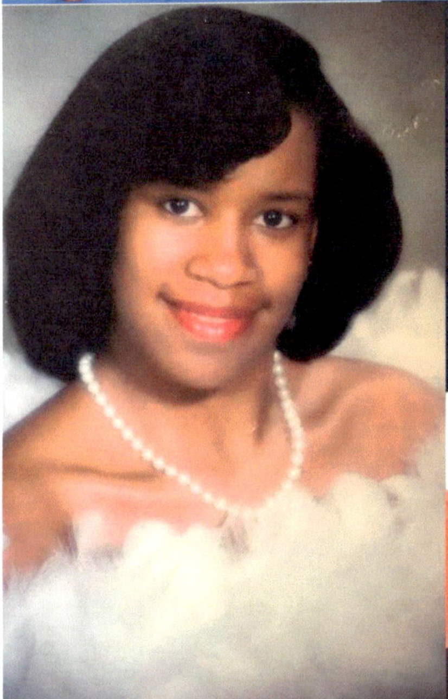

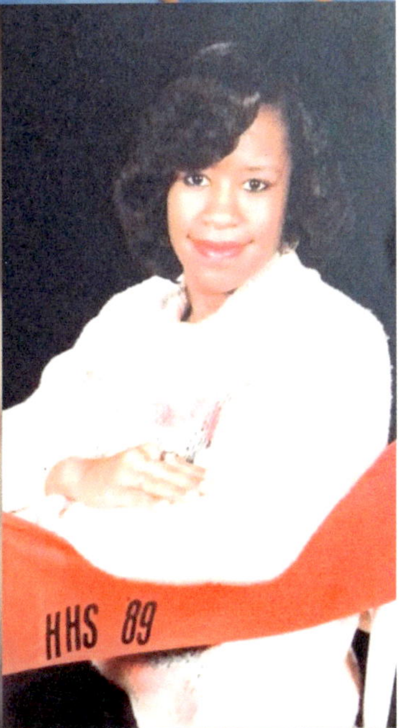
HHS 89

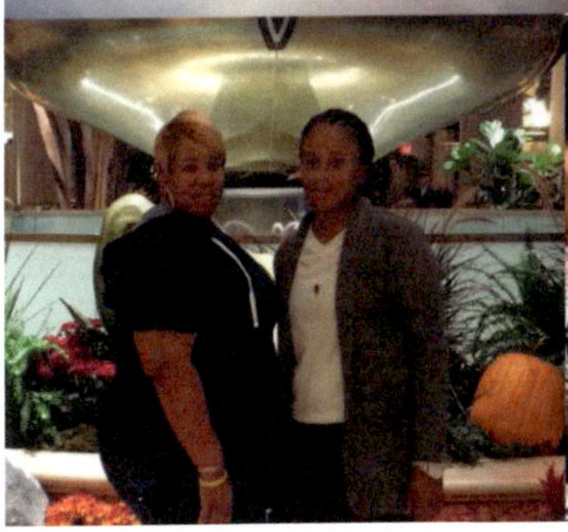

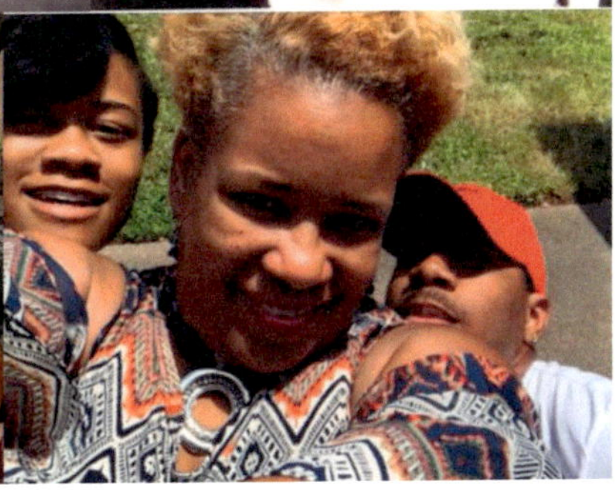

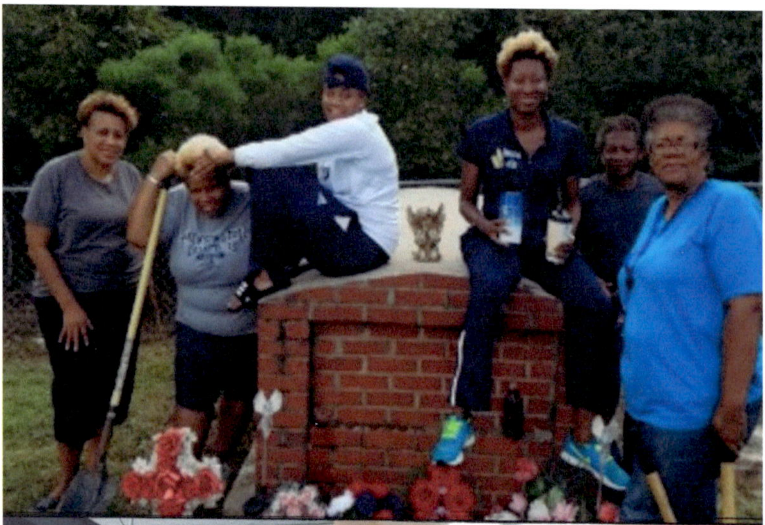
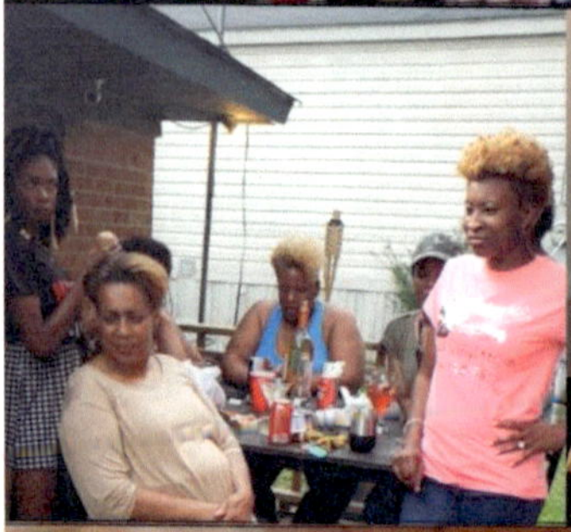
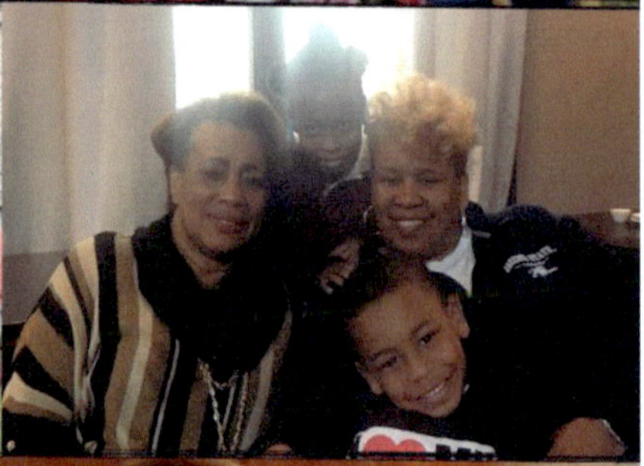
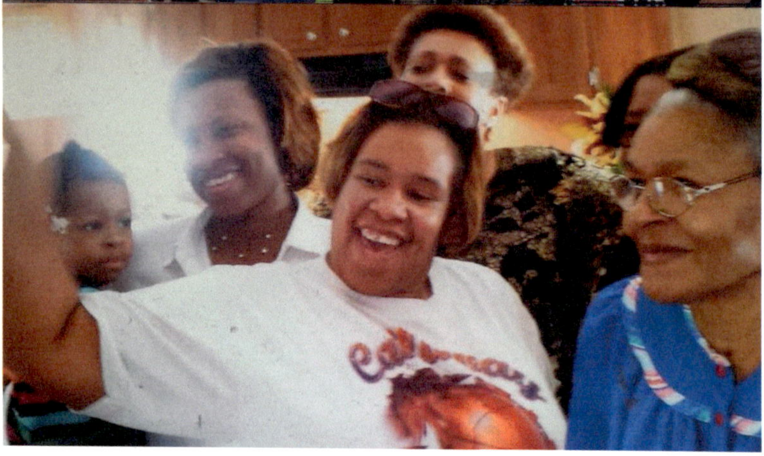

97

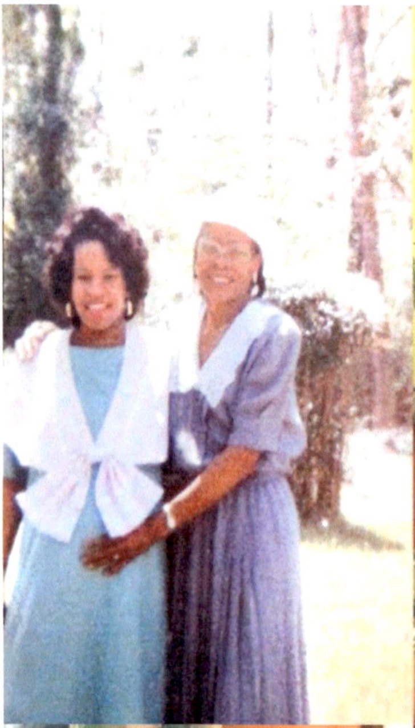

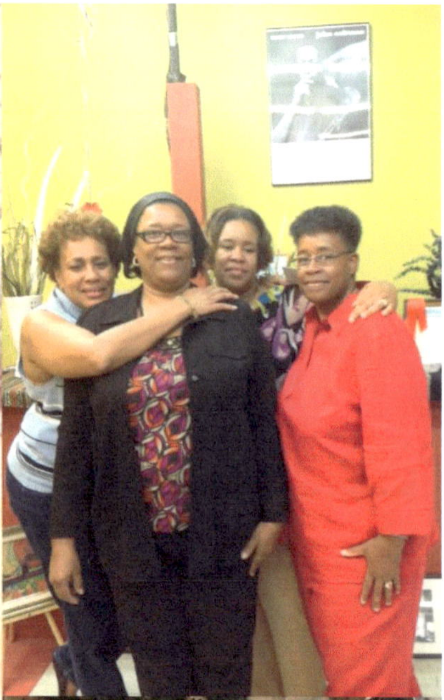

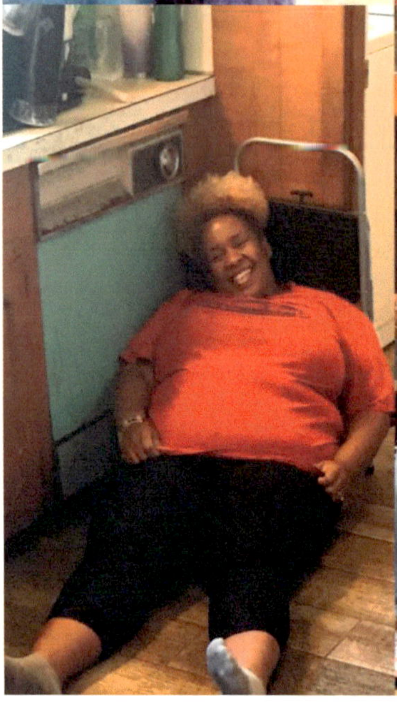

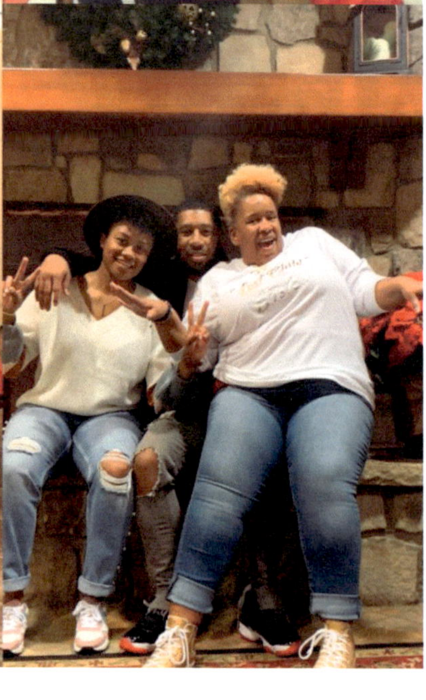

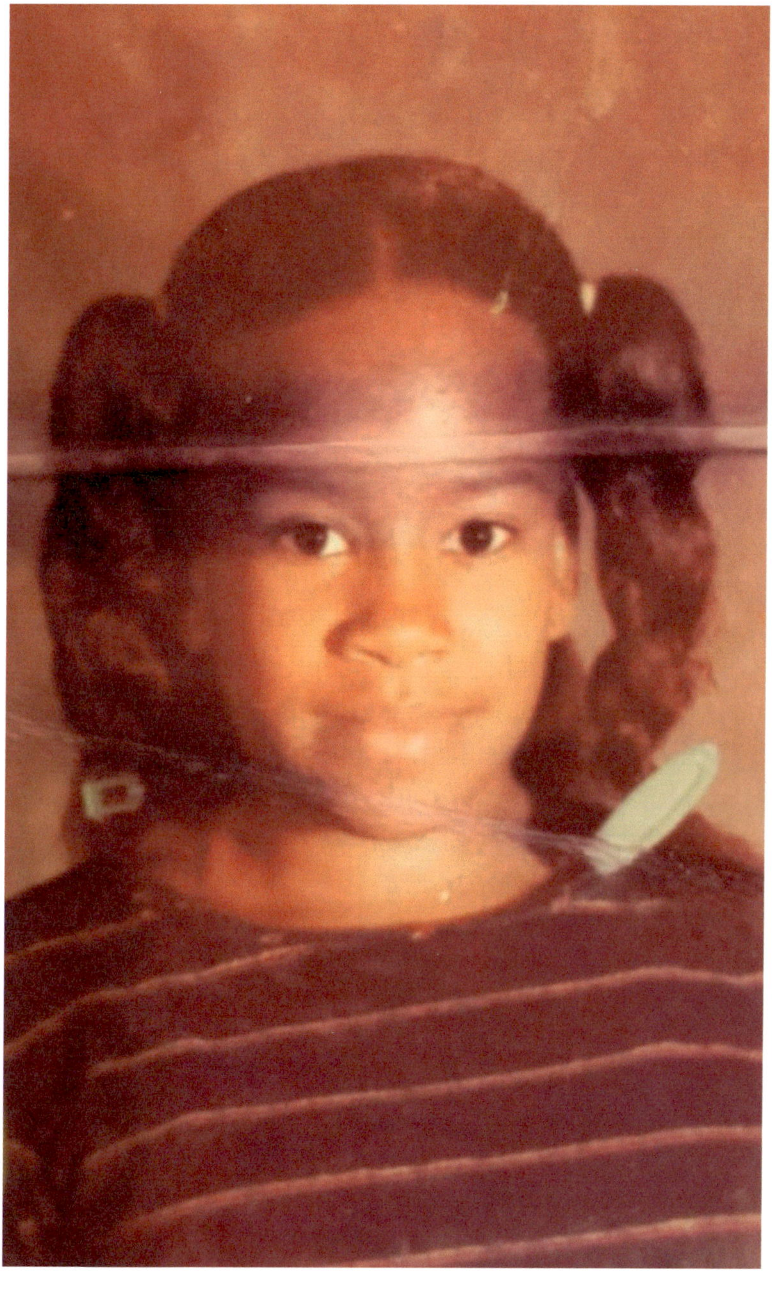

ABOUT THE AUTHOR

Alisa L. McGrew Ross, a first-time author with a wealth of experience in basketball and therapeutic recreation. With a Master's degree in Sport Science and a Bachelor's degree in Physical Education & Recreation, specializing in Therapeutic Recreation, Alisa brings a unique perspective to her writing.

Her basketball career started at the age of four and continued through college, where she achieved remarkable success. Alisa has received numerous accolades, including Rookie of the Year, Best Defensive Player, Most Valuable Player, and the Dandy Dozen Award. In her debut book, "The Game Savior," Alisa shares her deep connection to the game and showcases how basketball became her tool for overcoming life's trials. This nonfiction masterpiece will leave you motivated, moved, and ready to conquer your own game of life.

Made in the USA
Columbia, SC
25 January 2024